CHAPTER 14

Author Anajah Wade

EPPS
CREATIVEMINDZ
ENTERPRISE, LLC

Epps Creativemindz Publishing
ISBN-10: 0998056774
ISBN-13: 978-0-9980567-7-7

Copyright © 2017

Acknowledgements:

First off, I would like to thank the Lord for giving me the words to write and especially for giving me this gift of poetry. I put him first in all that I do! I would next like to thank Mrs. Epps for taking time out her busy schedule to help me with my first book. It has really been a blessing to work with her. She's such a kindhearted person and I am just so grateful to have worked with her.

Next, I would like to thank my family. My aunt, Ina Wade, my sister, Aniya Wade, my brother, Demetrius Kelly, and my grandmother Gloria Hooks. They have really pushed me and believed in me through all of this. When I first starting writing poetry I didn't think I was very good at it until my grandmother told me how much a poem I read to her, had blessed her. There was also a time that I wanted to stop writing but my aunt Ina and my former teacher Mrs. Sessoms, really kept pushing me and never gave up on this talent of mine. The two of them we're there for me when I thought I had nobody else and I truly do appreciate them so much. I would also like to thank my mother, Kristy Lindsay and my father, Lewis Wade.

I would also like to acknowledge my pastor for encouraging me as well. He has also allowed me to recite a few of my poems at church and I am so grateful to have him as a pastor. He has inspired me in so many ways. I've always wanted to be book writer, so I am so grateful to be able to have this great opportunity because most people don't.

The Essence of My Emotions:

Sometimes I start to feel dark and all alone;
Just praying and meditating on getting back to my comfort
zone.

Lots of things go on behind closed doors;
But nobody ever knows!

When things start to go left;
You realize many different things like who really cares and
the people that's been there.

I just hope for better days;
And for this strong pain to go away, but it just hasn't.

If you know the real me, then you know it takes a lot to
bring me down;
But it really hurts!

Have you ever had a bad dream, full of lots of bad things?
Well that's my life!

Sticks and stones scraping against my bones;
Because words do hurt!

I close my eyes and try to escape;
I tell the Lord that my soul, is ready for him to take.

Poetry is how I escape from all these things;
It helps calm my nerves and express my pain.

So, when my heart starts to hurt;
I give birth to a new poetry verse to show that this pain
doesn't define me!

I am a gift from above;
God blessed me with this gift from above!

So, don't feel anyway if you see me cry;
It's a sign that I'm making it!

Bows before Bros:

In middle school I would always cheer.
It seemed as if they were some of the best and worse years.

The smiles, the routines, and everything in between.
I loved it. I still do, actually!

I miss doing sports in school;
But my academics are more important!

Cheerleading was my first love!
I will always miss it.

It's the feeling after a game;
When little kids you don't even know
Come up to you and already know your name.

It's that feeling;
When other little girls say they want to be like you.

Being a cheerleader comes with a lot of good influencing
too.

The thing I love most about cheering;
Was having something to work for.

Sometimes it was hard;
So I had to work even harder.

I love cheering;
I will never forget to put bows before bros

Yo-yo:

We sometimes go through moments in life;
Where we're up or we're down.

You know, situations that try to hinder us or keep us bound.
But I refuse to always have a frown, or keep my head
down.

The devil's schemes can sometimes have us feeling like a
yo-yo!

His plans, his plots, and his schemes;
Can sometimes have us doing so many things.

God allowed us to make it through;
He stated that we are royalty, and children of the highest
too.

So, he keeps me up!

No matter how much the Devil tries to make us feel down;
God keeps our heads up and it isn't in his will for us to be
down!

Daughter to Mother:

Mommy you are a queen!
And to me, you mean everything.

Mommy you are royalty;
God only created one of you and I'm so grateful for him
doing that too.

Mommy, when you begin to feel down;
Just know, me as your daughter will always be there to pick
up your crown.

Mommy you are truly royalty;
Everything about you glistens and shines!

You're gorgeous, loving, God fearing, and so much more.
I love you mommy!

Love:

Everyone says that love is like a drug;
So, I try my best to stay away!

You inhale the deception of your deceiving so called
"significant other";
While you exhale the truth because your deeply in love.

And every time you inhale you become high off what you
think is love;
When all you want is someone who can meet your needs
And fulfill your sexual fantasies.

You desire to feel good but as we all know;
Drugs aren't good for you!

Love is as strong as any other drug;
Once you get on it, it's complicated to stop abusing the
substance.

So, I say to you be careful with this drug called love!

Black History:

Beaten, assaulted, and sentenced to death.
Chained up and punished for their master's wealth.

Dehumanized and treated like wild animals;
Some masters quoted bible scriptures and didn't see any
harm in these acts;
They even took pleasure looking at the wounds on their
backs.

They wanted to, but it was a risk to be free;
Cuz' they were treated like wild animals approaching
someone without a leash.

The pain, the suffering, and the loud cries at night!
Fredrick Douglass, Harriet Tubman took a stand for what
was right.

Fredrick said "How dare they celebrate while my brothers
and sisters are still slaves"
With the directions of God, slavery can go away.

Now we're here, free as can be;
If it wasn't for the lord, who knows where we would be?

Now no matter if you're Black, White, Hispanic or
anything else;
God made a way for us to all have success.

That comes to show how good God is and how much he
loves his kids.
So, when you start thinking that a situation is impossible to
get through;
Just know that God Not only made a way in February, but
in the other months too.

* * *

A way:

God made a way!
If it wasn't for him, who knows where we'd be today?

Defined by our Color;
Having to work the fields;
While our masters rejoiced with their significant others.

But God said "No, this shall not be."
"I sent my son for all those that believe."

"I even brought him back on the third day for their peace."
"This violence shall stop, it must flee!"

A Mother:

Mothers are usually seen as the women that has birthed a
baby;
My definition is far from this, so just hear me out!

A mother is a woman that pushes her kid(s) towards
success;
And she might even be heartbroken if her kid(s) show her
any less!

A mother is a special woman that wants to hear the voices
of her kid(s) everyday!

A mother is a woman that talks to the lord praying for her
kid(s);
Knowing her prayers won't go void.

A mother is a woman that picks her kid(s) up when they're
down!
And helps take away her kid's awful frown.

A mother is a woman that is not to be her kid's friend.
But to lead, guide, and stay with them till the end.

A mother isn't just a woman that pushes her kid(s);
But loves them like a mother should and always will!

Living Proof:

At a young age, I grew up way too fast!
I used to skip school, I didn't even want to attend class.

At the end of that school year;
I was looking at my grades, wondering how in the world I
passed.

Around this time, I was going through a lot at home;
I cried myself to sleep every night.

It seemed as if depression was an enemy I had to fight.

Growing up in a house of abuse;
I used to use my situation as an excuse.

Now I'm trying to be the living proof;
That it's not impossible to make it, for the other people that
are going through.

No longer will I use my pain as a way;
But as another reason to scream, shout, and rejoice unto the
lord.

When I was going through;
The lord brought me out alive!

I am so grateful to be here!

IF IT WAS EASY, EVERYONE WOULD DO IT.

Silence:

Sometimes I just think about the things I've been through.
Sometimes I just I hear voices, saying "Put the knife deep

in you".

If only I was aborted when I was young;
Then I wouldn't think about harming myself or stopping

the air from my lungs.

"The pain will be over, once you just slice your neck".
I say back to the voice "How hard is that?"

I want to be free, from all this pain and hurt;
I just want my body buried six feet under the dirt!

Nobody cares about me!
It's like being the black sheep of my family; is whom I'm
destined to be

Tears running from my check;
The desire to live is running away from me too.

Once I die, you're gonna' wish that you would've paid
attention
To all my mood swings and the deep dark things that I've
mentioned
It will be too late!

Oh no, don't you dare cry when you find out that I took my
own life;
Don't cry or think about what you should've did, at night.

● ● ●

Don't say "she was my friend, I loved her till the end".
If you loved me, why didn't it show?

Why didn't you come talk to me, when you witnessed me
crying up close?
Will my heart stop pumping, if I overdosed?
I think it will!

Just the thought of me popping pill after pill, fascinates me.
How will my body feel; when it has to flee?

Will I be sleep forever?
Will I be silenced?

THAT'S THE THING ABOUT PAIN, IT DEMANDS TO BE FELT.

JOHN GREEN

Soccer Girl:

Most people see soccer as just kicking a ball with your feet.
But I crave playing this sport every day of the week!

Most girls will go crazy if their eyebrows aren't on fleek.
But see me, I'd rather have a brand-new pair of cleats.

Soccer is what I love to do;
It's not just some game I play but it's a part of my life too.

Yes, I enjoy kicking balls for a sport!
Oh, how I love soccer!

I'm Hurting:

Sometimes I start to feel dark, gloomy, and all alone. Simply left with no place to call a comfort zone. People stare at me; well into my deep and dark soul but what they don't see, is the fact that I'm hurting!

So many times, you've taken advantage of me for your own personal use. In the back of my mind, it still feels like you will walk out of my life with no excuse. My soul is crying aloud to be accepted. But you didn't hear my loud cries cuz' I sleep through this deep dark depression of mine. I sleep so much cuz' I'm too weak to stand up in pain on my feet.

When you look at me, what do you see? Do you see the pain in me because I am truly hurting! I took a sip of your love and became drunk off of your actions. Your love has intoxicated me and poisoned my soul. I was desperate for your love and I couldn't get enough, until I took a sip of your trust and I also thought that I could never get enough. But I did!

Can't you see that I'm hurting?

Happy Father's Day to a Special Friend:

Today is the day that I acknowledge you for your woks;
I know sometimes I may have had an attitude and kind of
treat you like dirt.

But you were persistent because you stayed with me &
never gave up.

I know you're not perfect cuz' none of us are;
But on the days, I fell down, you were there to patch up my
scares.
And the love I have for you, is like the love rich men have
for their cars.

I know you haven't known me that long;
But it feels like I've known you forever.

I believe God placed you in my life;
To make it even better.

You may not know this;
But I look up to you like a dad!

And when you come visit us and have to go back home;
My heart really gets sad!

I would like to say happy Father's Day Cory.
You're truly a great one.

The War is Not Quite Won:

See back in the days our ancestors had to fight;
So that we could learn and have opportunities like the
white.

Rosa parks sat, so that Martin Luther could walk;
Martin Luther walked so that Obama could run;
Now people are killing each other for fun!

Did you know our ancestors were killed for our equal
rights?
Now we're too lazy to even pick up a pencil and write.

Get very ecstatic and pay very close attention, to what I am
about to mention;
God wants us to listen, which is why he gave the Quaker's
a powerful vision;

See, the Quaker's were a group of white people that
thought slavery was wrong;
So, they helped Harriet Tubman and the others move
through this underground Zone.

Lots of people died for our right to vote;
Now we're just sitting around, taking these elections as a
joke.

It's up to us to take a stand, if you don't want our country
to end up in the wrong hands.
I didn't mean to step on your toes or sound rude;
But God shared with us his vision and now it's time to see
it through.

Feelings:

Sometimes I just wonder what can I do…
For you to love me much as I love you.

Will you love me in the morning when my hair isn't done?
Would you love me during the rising of the sun?

When I'm way too weak to love myself;
Will you care for me, love me, and still be there?

The Lord is My Savior:

I have been patiently waiting and contemplating for a
change;
I even had to go through and experience many different
things!

Every night I pray for better;
Just hoping things will turn around like the weather!

There are times where I feel alone;
Just because I left my comfort zone

Temptation is a hard thing to pass;
So, I constantly read my bible, like it's my class.

Being a young Christian is very tuff!
Especially when it's so easy to get into the wrong stuff!

Every morning I wake up, breathing your air.
I am so thankful that you honestly care.

When I look over my shoulders;
I notice miracles all over.

If there's a day I don't wake up and give you praise;
I ask for your forgiveness, since I didn't handle my
business.

There are many things I ask of you;
But the things you expect from me, I barley ever do.

I just thank you for your love and your grace;
And for you keeping me safe, because you don't have to do
it!

Let your

FAITH

be bigger

than your

FEAR

AndreaReiser.com

Igniting the Fire:

I would like to thank my church;
Which is The Bread of Life.

For helping me give me life to Jesus Christ;

I grow and prosper as the day goes along;
I would like to thank God for helping me with this poem.

Fighting against spiritual hosts;
I get all my strength from the Holy Ghost.

With the help from my pastor;
I know God is my master.

And no matter how hard this war gets;
I promise I will never quit.

I am already victories;
So, I give God all the glory because he's worthy.

I am here to ignite my inner fire;
At a young age I already have a desire to be endowed by
his fire.

God gave us all a gift;
Not meant for waste!

"If you can't fly then run.
If you can't run then walk.
If you can't walk then crawl.
But whatever you do
you have to keep moving forward."

- Martin Luther King Jr.

www.ingramcontent.com/pod-product-compliance
Lightning Source LLC
Chambersburg PA
CBHW071807020426
42331CB00008B/2421